Bruce R. Joyce
Beverly Showers

POWER
IN STAFF DEVELOPMENT THROUGH RESEARCH ON TRAINING

About the Authors

Bruce R. Joyce is Visiting Professor, and Beverly Showers is Assistant Professor, both at the College of Education, University of Oregon, Eugene.

Copyright © 1983 by the Association for Supervision and Curriculum Development. All rights reserved. No part of this publication may be reproduced or transmitted in any form or by any means, electronic or mechanical, including photocopy, recording, or any information storage and retrieval system, without permission in writing from the publisher.

ASCD publications present a variety of viewpoints. The views expressed or implied in this publication are not necessarily official positions of the Association.

Price: $7.50
ASCD Stock Number: 611-83304
ISBN: 0-87120-121-6
Library of Congress
  Card Catalog Number: 83-73348

Contents

   Foreword v
1 The Integration of Research and Practice 1
2 Horizontal and Vertical Transfer 5
3 Attacking the Transfer Problem 11
4 Making Training More Effective 15
5 Parallels with Athletic Training 23
6 Increasing Learning Aptitude 27
   Appendix 33
   References 41

Foreword

What is the secret of excellence in teaching? Why does one teacher do extraordinarily well while another wallows in mediocrity?

Bruce Joyce and Beverly Showers have found that mastering alternative models of teaching helps build competence and effectiveness in the repertoire of classroom teachers. High quality training is the precursor to superior results. Only by applying knowledge derived from research on training in other fields can staff developers help teachers develop their own personal technology of teaching.

The attainment of new skills, however, does not by itself ensure transfer to classroom use. Joyce and Showers contend that teacher training programs should incorporate study of the transfer process itself. Trainers and teachers must understand that the more important it is to learn a new skill, the greater will be the discomfort in learning it.

These principles require team effort. Effective training programs exist and many more can exist. It is up to instructional leaders to provide the necessary support and to create the appropriate climate and settings.

Lawrence S. Finkel,
ASCD President, 1983-84

1

The Integration of Research and Practice

With half-formed aspirations and ideals, teacher candidates are touched briefly by training and then are set, Candide-like, on the seas of the classroom where they struggle for competence (Ryan, 1980). They learn their craft in unbelievable solitude inside their "cells" in the honeycomb of the school (Joyce and Clift, 1983; Lortie, 1975). The fortunate ones find a mentor, usually a more experienced person just down the hall. But these mentors are busy, too, and the help most teachers get even from their closest colleagues is meager (Arends, 1982; Joyce, Bush, and McKibbin, 1982).

Because teachers learn to manage the tasks of teaching by virtue of their own ingenuity, it is not surprising that they see teaching as an individualistic act. Schools provide little time for collective planning. Leadership in most schools is oriented toward the day-to-day problems of management and logistics (Leithwood and Montgomery, 1982). Teachers have little chance to learn the skills of collaborative action, so they are reluctant to give up their limited bits of free time to the vague promises of collaborative activity (Lortie, 1975). From time to time, snatches of "staff development" activities touch their lives, usually in brief workshops (Gall, 1982; Mertens and Yarger, 1981). But in any given year the average teacher in the United States participates in only about three days of inservice work, rarely more than a day at a time, and usually in brief workshops that feature "inspiring" speeches and demonstrations of discrete skills.

We would change all that. We would build a synergistic environment where collaborative enterprises are both normal and sustaining and where continuous training and study both of academic substance and the craft of teaching are woven into the fabric of the school, bringing satisfaction by virtue of an increasing sense of growth and competence. Thus, we envision a major change in the ecology of professional life.

To begin with, it is plain from the research on training that teachers can be wonderful learners. They can master just about any kind of teaching strategy or implement almost any kind of sensible curriculum—if the appropriate conditions are provided. It is also clear that those who criticize the motivations of teachers, worry about their willingness and ability to learn, or believe that the only way to improve the teaching profession is to change its personnel, are fundamentally wrong. High-quality training will give excellent results. Important new learning involves pain, and teachers are well able to withstand the discomfort. In many quarters teachers have been undersold as learners simply because inadequate training has been provided.

Let us consider the case of a new member of the Inland School faculty:

Sharlene Daniels is in her fifth year of teaching. During her first four years she worked in Rolling Hills, a suburb of a small city. Rolling Hills had a reputation as a very good district and a fine place to work. The district inservice program in Rolling Hills consisted of three one-day workshops, and the board of education was proud that they had been able to persuade the community that the two days that they closed school each year for the workshops would pay off for the district in the long run.

The first staff development day took place just before school opened, the second in November, and the third in March. Rolling Hills hired well-known consultants, who generally brought a complete day's set of activities with them. Sometimes, however, they would start things off with an inspirational speaker in the morning and then have consultants for the elementary, middle, and high school for the rest of the day. Sharlene heard several fine speeches and watched a host of performers present their methods for teaching the various elementary and secondary subjects. When she tried their ideas in her classroom, however, she became very frustrated. What had sounded so good and looked so reasonable didn't work out very well in her hands.

Her principal looked in on her regularly and praised her orderly, attractive classroom and her good ideas for teaching reading.

At the end of her first year she enrolled in a reading clinic at a nearby university. For eight weeks, she studied with the team of teachers that operated the clinic and took courses in the diagnosis and remediation of reading disabilities. Sharlene thought that her strengths were in the content areas of social studies, science, and literature, but her principal was concerned with how she taught reading and arithmetic and didn't seem particularly interested in her ideas for teaching reading through the content areas.

Nonetheless, by the end of her fourth year of teaching, Sharlene was comfortable. She had learned the role of teacher as it was acted out at Rolling Hills. Still, she was able to back off from the role a bit and reflect on the school and the education it was providing its students. She wondered how the school could be regarded as one of the best in the area when science, mathematics, social studies, creative writing, and literature were missing from the curriculum. She realized that she was working in a very pleasant, but very limited environment where the skills of reading and arithmetic were dominant, but where the reading and writing was not very literary and the arithmetic not very mathematical.

At a weekend science workshop she became acquainted with some of the members of the Inland School faculty in another school district. She noticed that they had come to the workshop as a team and that they were gathering materials and making plans for their workshops back at Inland. They let her join them. Later, she visited the Inland school and watched that team and others at work, teaching before each other, offering advice and experimenting together.

When an opening at Inland appeared, Sharlene applied for it on an impulse, was interviewed, and accepted. The members of the team to which she was assigned explained that she would have a "coaching partner" and that she and that partner would visit each other, watch each other teach, and give each other assistance. They also had to agree on one or two teaching strategies that they would focus on each year and make a commitment to master them and experiment with them in the classroom.

Before the first workshop, Sharlene was given curriculum materials and an explanation of the rationale behind the teaching strategy approach that was to be used. The first workshop was devoted almost entirely to a discussion of the uses of the strategy, the theory behind it, and how various children responded to it. Sharlene was surprised, because she thought the workshop would be devoted to demonstrations. However, those were reserved for the workshop's second session: The Inland consultant demonstrated the teaching strategy, teaching the teachers the same kinds of lessons they would later be teaching to children. Several of the team members were uncomfortable with science, so the consultant decided that it was important for those persons to become familiar with the learner's role in the teaching strategy because they would soon be teaching their children those same roles. At the end of the workshop, the consultant did a careful demonstration with a group of children. She explained the teaching strategy to both the children and the teachers and, after the children had gone, they discussed the lesson and how it could be adapted to various groups of children. For the next workshop, Sharlene found that *she* was expected to prepare a lesson and teach it to her fellow teachers.

At that workshop, Sharlene and the rest of her team took turns teaching one another. Thus, she got to see the other teachers practice the strategy. Her team then made plans to try a couple of prototype lessons for their students over the next two weeks. Those two weeks were very uncomfortable ones for Sharlene. Things did not go quite as planned. She found herself thinking she already had developed several fine ways of teaching and wondering why she should go to the trouble of learning these new methods, especially if it was going to be painful to learn them. Her coaching partner laughed when Sharlene shared her thoughts and explained that everyone felt the same way. They had learned that it wasn't too hard to understand any new teaching strategy and to develop a certain skill with it, but until they had tried it a dozen or so times, they all felt varying degrees of discomfort. "The better you are," explained her partner, "the worse you feel, because you're used to having things go well. Actually, things probably are going well, but you just don't feel as comfortable as you did teaching in the ways that have become familiar to you."

Sure enough, after five or six tries with the children Sharlene began to feel much more comfortable. She was actually able to get the children to engage in inductive thinking and it excited them. Then the teachers began to demonstrate for one another. Soon she found herself in the library after school teaching a group of her students surrounded by a ring of her fellow teachers. She had watched the other teachers occupy the same position, but this was her first time and she felt like a child on the first day of school. After the children left, she was surprised that no one made critical comments. Then she suddenly realized that none of them ever made critical comments to one another. Instead, they offered suggestions. More important, most of the discussion that followed came after a comment by one of the teachers whom Sharlene had felt looked the most confident and even nonchalant in the workshop settings. "You just showed me a new level of that lesson," she said. "I've been doing all right and thought I had it right, but the way you handled that teaching strategy gave me a lot of ideas that I can use to make it a lot stronger than I believed it was."

Sharlene was learning what it meant to go from a school with a minimal curriculum and a minimal inservice program to a school where the faculty had learned how to train themselves to make curriculum changes for the school as a whole and to add new teaching techniques to their individual repertoires.

After a couple of months, during which each teacher tried the new strategies a dozen times or more, they began to feel "possession" of the strategy. Then initial discomfort passed to a feeling of strength and power. They owned a new tool and it became part of their "natural" repertoire.

The Inland team is engaged in the serious study of alternative models of teaching (Joyce and Weil, 1980), using training procedures that enable them to bring almost any approach to teaching within their grasp. The elements they use include:
- the study of the theoretical basis or the rationale of teaching method
- the observation of demonstrations by persons who are relatively expert in the model
- practice and feedback in relatively protected conditions (such as trying out the strategy on each other and then children who are relatively easy to teach)
- coaching one another as they work the new model into their repertoire, providing companionship, helping one another to learn to teach the appropriate responses to their students and to figure out the optimal uses of the model in their courses, and providing one another with ideas and feedback.

In previous reviews (Joyce and Showers, 1981, 1982), we have accumulated reports of research into the effects of each of these components on the development of skill in the use of a new approach to teaching and on the transfer of that approach into one's active teaching repertoire. The study of theory, the observation of demonstrations, and practice with feedback, taken together (provided they are of high quality), are sufficient to enable most teachers to develop skill to the point where they can, when called upon to do so, use the model fluidly and appropriately. However, the development of skill alone does not ensure transfer. Relatively few persons, having mastered a new teaching skill, will then transfer that skill into their active repertoire. *In fact, few will use it at all* (Showers, 1982). Continuous practice, feedback, and the companionship of coaches is essential to enable even *highly motivated* persons to bring additions to their repertoire under effective control.

To master a single teaching strategy, the procedures used by the Inland team are much more complex and extensive than common staff development procedures. Yet anything short of that effort will, for most people, fall short of its objective. Why is this so? We think the answer is in the nature of the process of transfer—of building competence in complex teaching skills to the point where they are incorporated into the teaching repertoire.

2

Horizontal and Vertical Transfer

Classically, transfer refers to the effect of learning one kind of material or skill or the ability to learn something new. When practice in one kind of athletic skill increases ability to learn another, *transfer* is occurring. Teaching, by its nature, requires continuous adaptation; it demands new learning in order to solve the problems of each moment and situation. Teaching skills and strategies are designed to help teachers solve problems—to reach students more effectively. To master a new teaching strategy, a teacher needs first to develop *skill* in the strategy. This can be accomplished in a training setting, such as a workshop. Then, the teacher needs to acquire executive control over the strategy, including the ability to use it appropriately and to adapt it to the students and classroom setting. Sometimes the achievement of executive control requires extensive amounts of new learning that can only be accomplished through practice in the classroom. It is at this phase of the mastery of the new strategy that the distinction between horizontal and vertical transfer becomes important.

Horizontal transfer refers to a condition in which a skill can be shifted directly from the training situation in order to solve problems. *Vertical* transfer refers to conditions in which the new skill cannot be used to solve problems unless it is adapted to fit the conditions of the workplace—that is, an extension of learning is required *before* problems can be solved effectively. Vertical transfer is more likely when: the context of training and the conditions of the workplace are different; a given skill is different from one's existing repertoire and does not fit easily into it; or additional understanding is needed to achieve executive control over the skill.

When the work and training settings are virtually identical, a skill often can be transferred from the training setting to the workplace "as is" with little additional learning on the job (horizontal transfer). For example, carpenters who learn to use a handsaw in a woodshop can, on the job, recreate the conditions of the shop almost exactly and apply their skill very much as it was learned in the training setting. When a new technique is introduced, carpenters can add it to their repertoire without much additional learning. The chief problem is integrating the new skill into existing patterns of behavior. Vertical transfer, however, involves differences in context so sufficient that new learning has to take place as the skill is transferred into the work situation. The additional learning has to occur in the work setting. In a real sense, the trainee must repossess the skill in the work context.

Examples of the vertical transfer problem abound in fields like counseling and teaching. In training settings, counselors can be introduced to the theory of an approach, it can be demonstrated for them, and they can practice it under simulated conditions. However, when they try to apply this skill in the workplace, they have the clients' needs, characteristics, and course of therapy to contend with. Counselors cannot simply go out and practice skill "X" whether or not the client needs it; they have to wait for the appropriate opportunity and exercise judgment about when and how to employ the skill. In addition, while the counselor can be taught to recognize variations in clients and general principles for adapting the skill to different clients, clients come in very great variety. The use of the skill requires counselors to learn about their clients, enter their frames of reference, and adjust the skill to their needs. In other words, to use the skill effectively, it must be transformed to "fit" the situation.

The distinction between horizontal and vertical transfer refers to the amount of learning and repossession of the skill that is necessary if it is to be functional in the work situation. When the skill just "slides" from training place to workplace, we say that the process is horizontal. When additional learning is required to transfer the skill, we speak of the process as vertical.

An important factor is the degree to which the new skill disrupts existing patterns of performance. Familiarity is the key here. The greater the degree to which a new skill fits into already familiar patterns, the less adjustment is needed. For example, imagine a primary teacher who employs Cuisenaire rods to teach mathematics concepts and definitions and who organizes the students into small groups to work with the rods. If that teacher is then introduced to the use of the abacus, he or she will need much less adjustment than a teacher who never uses concrete aids. The nonuser will have fewer existing behaviors to draw on and may have to develop a new pattern of organization as well (such as organizing groups of students to use the new material). In other words, the second teacher will probably have more skills to develop and more adjustments to make in order to be able to use the skill effectively.

Developing Executive Control

The conditions of performance can be divided into two categories—those in which the circumstances of performance *demand* the utilization of the skills and those in which the skills are brought into play as a consequence of a judgment made by the performer. In military and industrial settings, considerable effort has been expended in the development of "standard operating procedures"—that is, sequences of skills that have been previously organized for each worker. For example, during the training of infantry platoons procedures are developed for dispersing personnel, for organizing them to bring their fire to bear on given targets, for developing clear fields of fire, and for advancing on a target while keeping dispersed and under cover.

As much as possible, standard operating procedures include directions about when to bring to bear a cluster of relevant skills. In other words, a shifting and changing scene of events is reduced as much as possible to sets of operations that can be brought into play when the appropriate cues appear in the environment. General principles are formulated and taught so as to activate the skills. In the training of pilots, sets of skills are clustered around the elements of a flight plan and are brought to bear on demand. Entering the cockpit, the flight personnel know what to do to check out the equipment and instruments in the aircraft, communicate with the control tower, and leave the parking space. Another set of skills is brought into play to bring the aircraft to the edge of the runway, yet another to obtain clearance and propel the aircraft into flight. Other sets of closely monitored skills are brought to bear to carry out the flight plan and bring the aircraft to a safe landing.

The more closely the skills are identified and the principles governing their use defined, the less the trainees are permitted to use their own discretion. For example, factory workers are organized to the point where judgment is exercised as little as possible and breakdowns are referred to supervisory personnel.

Teaching is an occupation where the personnel operate with relatively little surveillance and few standard operating procedures. For example, a teacher of English has considerable latitude about the literary works that will be studied, the concepts that will be emphasized, the relationship between the study of literature and the study of writing, the teaching strategies that will be used, and the methods of evaluation that will be exercised. As presently organized, the tasks of teaching are not composed, as are the tasks of factory workers, of sets of objective-related activities to be called up in sequence according to predetermined principles. Consequently, the content of the training of teachers cannot be organized just by referring to a set of standard operating procedures. When a teacher is taught a range of teaching strategies and the appropriateness of those strategies to various kinds of objectives and students, the transfer of those skills into the workplace is largely under the governance of that individual teacher.

Teaching behavior *can* be more closely prescribed when highly detailed curriculum plans and elaborate training programs have been designed to prepare teachers to engage in highly standardized activities. However, in most phases of their work, teachers have wide latitude and work under little surveillance (Miles, 1981). Their training must provide them with a usable repertoire, not simply prepare them to implement a set of pre-defined operations.

In the phases of work where competence is derived from one's judgment-controlled repertoire, the effective use of a skill depends on what we term "executive control." Executive control consists of understanding the purpose and rationale of the skill and knowing how to adapt it to students, apply it to subject matter, modify or create instructional materials attendant to its use, organize students to use it, and blend it with other instructional approaches to develop a smooth and powerful whole.

Showers' (1982) recent study of teachers learning to use several models of teaching previously unfamiliar to them has provided new insight into the process of developing executive control during the period when vertical transfer is being accomplished. Showers' teachers were able to develop skill in the training situation with little apparent difficulty (see the discussion in Chapter 4 of the training components necessary for skill development). As they began to practice the strategies in their classrooms it became apparent that they needed help less with the observable skills for implementing the models than with the thinking processes necessary to use them effectively. The attainment of executive control became the major content of the coaching process that assisted them to transfer their skills to the workplace.

Teachers otherwise positive toward the content and process of their training and willing to practice the new teaching models in their classrooms, but who could not think conceptually about what they taught, and how and why, were apparently unable to use the new models successfully during the teaching of the experimental unit used as a transfer task for all teachers.

Teachers who did not, or could not, use the new strategies during the transfer task (a social studies unit focused on the town of Roussillon, France) rarely cited difficulty in thinking of ways to use the models as the reason for their failure to do so. Instead, they tended to mention time pressures or technical deficiencies. An examination of the lesson plans and interview data, however, revealed interesting differences in the organizational approaches taken to the material. While "low-transfer" teachers aimed toward mastery of factual lists (the climate, crops, occupations, and so on of Roussillon), "high-transfer" teachers focused on objectives, such as a "comparison of social mores in Roussillon-Eugene" and the "effects of Roussillon's economic system on politics and family life." Apparently, the high-transfer teachers could readily find appropriate uses for teaching strategies that stressed conceptual and analogic student thinking. The executive control they developed with the new teaching strategies appeared to be an essential ingredient in the successful transfer of their training to the classroom.

Discomfort: A Problem Created by Effective Training

During transfer, many teachers experience some degree of discomfort for several reasons. To begin with, learning to use new skills involves greater effort than the use of old ones. Second, new skills "feel" more awkward and less neutral than familiar ones for some time. Third, the use of an important new skill involves some risk. Instruction may go less smoothly until the new skill is mastered. Until executive control is achieved, the use of the skill can be confusing and laborious. The more important the skill, the more powerful it is, the greater the discomfort will be because it disrupts more behavior than a trivial skill.

Discomfort reduces the pleasure of practice and leads to avoidance because using the new skill can be more painful than continuing familiar ones. Thus, the teacher who needs the most practice—the one for whom the vertical path will be steepest—is the one most likely to avoid that practice.

Attacking the Transfer Problem

We believe that the "problem" of transfer is actually a new stage of learning that becomes a problem only if it is not recognized. The learning process does not stop once a teaching skill has been obtained. That skill must be transformed when it is transferred into one's active teaching repertoire. The conditions of the classroom are sufficiently different from training situations that one cannot simply walk from the training session into the classroom with the skill completely ready for use. It has to be changed to fit classroom conditions. The appropriate use of the skill in its context also requires that an understanding of the students, subject matter, the objectives to be achieved, and the dimensions of classroom management all be under "executive" control, that is, clearly understood so that skill can be used appropriately and forcefully.

All of us are less skillful with a model of teaching that is new to us than we are with the ones we have been using for some time. Successful transfer requires a period of labor during which the skill is practiced in its context until it is tuned to the same level of fluidity as the rest of one's repertoire. To confound things somewhat further, sets of teaching behaviors that surround and make one's existing repertoire function well may actually prove dysfunctional when new models of teaching are added to the store house of skills.

For example, suppose a teacher who is accustomed to running brisk and pointed "drill and practice" sessions begins to learn how to work inductively with students. The swift pace of the drill and practice, the directive feedback to the students, and the ability to control the content and movement of the lesson are at first somewhat dysfunctional as the teacher assumes a less assertive stance, relies more on the students' initiative, probes their understanding, and helps them learn to give one another feedback. The new teaching strategy seems awkward. Its pace seems slow. The teaching moves that served so well before now appear to retard the progress of the new kind of lesson. After a while, however, practice in context smooths off those rough edges and the new strategy gradually comes to feel as comfortable and "under control" as the old one did.

Of course, some people navigate the process of transfer easily, but for no one is it effortless. For most of us, vertical transfer requires substantial assistance. Let us see what we can do to attack the problem, to create conditions that will enable teachers to achieve vertical transfer with as much ease and power as possible.

Experience Outside of Education

In military, industrial, and medical applications trainers traditionally attack the problem of transfer in three ways. First, they attempt to bring training conditions as close as possible to an approximation of the work situation and emphasize the "overlearning" of skills. Second, they attempt to design the work situation to bring about demand conditions in which the routines of skills can be applied very much as they are learned. Third, they try to simplify the problem frame of the workplace whenever a repertory of new skills has to be learned.*

Bringing training in line with the conditions of the workplace. With the use of devices such as simulators, designers of training have attempted to provide circumstances in which skills can be practiced in situations as close as possible to those encountered in the workplace. In these training contexts, the study of theory, the use of modelling, and opportunities for practice with careful feedback are mixed in such a way as to bring the trainees to the highest possible level of skill. Then they are taught to apply the skill under realistic conditions.

The idea is to *minimize* the amount of new learning that has to take place during the process of transfer. Obviously, if the training conditions can be made exactly equal to the conditions of the workplace, and the trainee brought to the point where he or she can exercise a high level of skill in those training conditions, then the new learning required to bridge the gap to the workplace will be minimized. "Overlearning" means that supervised practice is continued *after* the point where an acceptable criterion of performance is achieved in order to develop really smooth processes that are very much under control.

Controlling the context of the workplace: Creation of "demand" conditions. In military, industrial, and commercial applications, considerable effort is exerted to provide *predictable* conditions of work so that the skills learned in

---

*For a discussion of occupational differences in conceptions of training and its practice, see Joyce and Clift, 1983.

training can be put into place with minimum disruption. Assembly lines, for example, are organized in such a way as to minimize unpredictable events. Detailed work plans are developed and control mechanisms put in place to ensure that they will be carried out. In a curious kind of way, this serves to make the workplace an extension of the training setting, and in fact training is used as one of the mechanisms for controlling the workplace.

Pilot training is a good example. Pilots are taught how and when to behave in certain kinds of ways in training and are not expected to invent different kinds of sequences capriciously in the course of their work. They are, in fact, to make the workplace conform to the routines that have been learned during training. This again minimizes the problem of transfer; that is, it reduces it to one of horizontal rather than vertical transfer. Every possible behavior is in a sense programmed, and the necessary skills for exercising those behaviors are taught in the training situation. Of course, pilots do face unpredictable conditions sometimes, and for these they are taught general principles involving the exercise of judgment and new learning as problems are being solved.

Similarly, business procedures are routinized. Accountants are not only taught how to set up accounting procedures but to exert control in the workplace so that those accounting procedures can in fact be implemented.

Controlling the problem setting where a judgment-applied repertoire is necessary. Most intricate, perhaps, are the attempts to simplify the setting for application when it is not possible to create a complete approximation of the workplace in the course of training.

Medicine provides a good example. Physicians are prepared with sets of skills and strategies for solving problems, many of them highly standardized. A mixture of practical experience and lectures, readings, demonstrations, and practice under close supervision is used to develop skills in those routines. However, the medical profession has no managers who attempt to provide a complete system for the practice of medicine or for its application in the workplace. Physicians make judgments about what skills in their repertoire they will apply in a particular work setting and when, and they assemble that repertoire as they deem it necessary in order to solve their problems.

What *is* done is to provide conditions under which the exercise of judgment can occur under optimal conditions. Generally speaking, physicians contact one patient at a time so they can concentrate on the symptoms of that patient. When working under emergency conditions, they can call on laboratories and deploy other personnel to carry out treatment. If puzzled, they can call on colleagues. These conditions do not eliminate the problem to transfer from the training situation into the workplace, but they do simplify it.

In emergency circumstances, doctors behave very much like workers in very complex factories, applying routines that have been organized well in advance to stop bleeding, restore breathing, and provide assistance to stabilize the human organism. In most of their practice, however, doctors work in a problem-simplifying situation that gives them the time to apply their repertoire in a relatively deliberate and judgmental fashion. Similarly, counselors work with one patient at a time or with small groups to establish programs that give them an opportunity to observe their clients and make decisions about which treatments to apply.

In contrast, teaching is a very confusing and difficult setting. The circumstances of young teachers are cases in point. There has been much attention recently to the stress beginning teachers experience in their early months and years of teaching. From a training point of view, this stress is not surprising at all. Even assuming that their training has been excellent, beginning teachers are thrust into a situation in which they have to organize up to six classes of children. They select the content to be taught and the teaching strategies and instructional materials to be used; they learn to manage children, handle behavior problems, and relate to parents, and they struggle to get along with both administrators and peers—all of this in circumstances in which they meet their clients in large groups where the stimuli for individuals are mixed with those of many others.

Moreover, they work in a field where many types of problems and situations are not approached systematically through training, so they have to manufacture solutions to many problems on the spot. Under these conditions, transfer is extremely difficult. Excellent training may have provided them with a fine teaching strategy, but it will be good for only certain purposes. They have to decide on an appropriate occasion for using the strategy, adjust it for not one but 20 to 30 clients, and gain their on-the-job practice while engaging in a large number of other complex tasks.

Making Training More Effective

The basic problem is the acquisition of ideas and skills and obtaining executive control over them—the expansion of professional competence and its application in a complex situation.

What can be done? We propose that the following elements be included in training programs:

1. Forecasting the problem of transfer throughout the training process.
2. Developing very high degrees of skill prior to classroom practice.
3. Providing explicitly for executive control.
4. Providing for practice in the workplace immediately following skill development.
5. Providing for "coaching" by peers as vertical transfer is being accomplished.
6. Generating a "learning how to learn" effect.

These should not be implemented separately and, as we will see, require a quite different attitude toward training than has been common in the past, but each contributes distinctively to the achievement of our goal.

Forecasting the Problem of Transfer

The first step is to teach everyone involved in training about the problem of transfer and what they can do to overcome it. The trainees must be made aware of what is involved in horizontal transfer. Failure to forecast transfer is one of the reasons why teacher candidates develop the view that the first components of their training programs are "theoretical" and useless. It is a mistake for teachers to believe that if they attend a workshop, even where a skill is explained, demonstrated, and practiced, that they will need no further learning to bring the skill under control.

Teacher trainees must be mentally and emotionally prepared to engage in the practice necessary to permit new learning to take place. Even experienced teachers will find themselves uncomfortable with a new skill for some time for the reasons we have already described. They will have much less control over the new skill than the skills in their existing repertoire, and consequently they will feel less competent with it. The skills that surround the new skill in action will also need to be adjusted or "reprogrammed" in order to minimize interference from them.

The teacher must accept responsibility for the struggle to achieve transfer. To ease the struggle, the first step is to develop an understanding of the process of transfer and accept the challenge it presents. The experience of the approximately five percent of teachers who have managed to incorporate new teaching strategies into their repertoires without assistance has much to tell us. Several who we have interviewed indicate that they are well aware of what is involved. They forecast the problem for themselves and consciously push themselves through the period of discomfort, deliberately altering customary patterns to accommodate the new skills and viewing the dislocation of familiar skills as a challenge to be overcome.

Developing a High Degree of Skill

A major part of the attack is the development of a *high degree* of skill in the training setting. Quite simply, it is not reasonable to expect poorly developed skills to be transferred. Thorough training conducted in an adequate time frame is essential. While there are quite a number of formulations of training elements, four conditions appear to be both necessary to and adequate for the development of job-related skills in most vocations and professions. The first of these is the exploration of the theory of the skill through lectures, discussions, readings, and so forth. The trainee is brought to an understanding of the rationale behind the skill, why it is constructed as it is, how it is used in the workplace, and the principles that govern its use. Study of theory facilitates skill acquisition by increasing one's discrimination of the demonstrations, by providing a mental image to guide practice and clarify feedback, and by promoting the attainment of executive control.

Second is the demonstration of the skill or its modelling. Although the mechanisms by which modelling works are not clearly understood, skill development is greatly facilitated by seeing demonstrations of it. Skills can be demonstrated in settings that simulate the workplace, mediated through film or videotape, or conducted live in the training setting. Demonstrations can be mixed with explanation; the theory and modelling components need not be conducted separately. In fact, they have reciprocal effects. Mastery of the rationale of the skill facilitates discrimination, and modelling facilitates the understanding of underlying theories by illustrating them in action.

The third component is practice of the skill under simulated conditions. The closer the training setting approximates the workplace the more transfer is facilitated. Considerable amounts of skill can be developed, however, in settings far removed from and different from the workplace. "Peer-teaching," practice with other teachers, even has advantages. It provides experience as a "student," enables trainees to profit from one another's ideas and skill, and clarifies mistakes. It also is a good arrangement in which to develop the skills of peer coaching. Peer teaching and practice with small groups of children are safer settings for exploration than a full classroom. How much practice is needed depends, of course, on the complexity of the skill. The more simple skills, or those most similar to previously developed ones, will require less practice than those that are more complex or different from the teacher's current repertoire.

Finally, feedback about performance greatly facilitates skill development. Trainees can learn to provide feedback to each other and, utilizing audio or video recordings, can critique themselves once they have a clear idea of the skill and how to use it.

Mediated packages have been developed that provide presentations of theory, demonstrations, and instructions on how to practice and obtain feedback. A motivated trainee can learn a relatively simple skill on his or her own. Complex skills or models of teaching, however, generally require training staff to demonstrate, provide feedback, and help the trainees visualize implementation.

When a new skill fits easily into a trainee's existing repertoire, the development of a high degree of skill is in itself sufficient to bring about transfer by a motivated learner. When the skill involves an expansion of one's repertoire, however, further training in the workplace is necessary for most trainees if they are to gain control of the skill. Even horizontal transfer demands the attainment of a much higher degree of skill than has been customary in most training applications in teacher education.

Our current rule of thumb is that trainees learning a new teaching strategy probably need 15 to 20 demonstrations over the course of the training sequence and a dozen or more opportunities to practice the skill. Sharan and Hertz-Lazarowitz (1982), in a program designed to teach a new and complex teaching strategy to a group of Israeli teachers, provided 60 hours of theory, demonstration, practice, and feedback in one year before instituting a combination consultant and peer-coaching treatment to facilitate transfer of the new strategy to the workplace in the following year. One- or two-day workshops simply do not provide enough time to develop the degree of competence necessary for most trainees to be able to apply a new skill in the work setting.

Executive Control

Important skills cannot be used mindlessly, and principles need to be developed in the training setting concerning the appropriate use of the skill, how to modify it to fit the students, how to tell when it is working, and how to read one's own behavior and the behavior of the students to determine the degree to which it is effective. Principles for executive control provide teachers with the intellectual scaffolding necessary to understand the skill and its appropriate use and to discriminate elements of the skill from one another. During practice in the workplace, the teacher uses these principles to judge appropriate use and decides how to modify behavior to accommodate the students. Not until the teacher can select the strategy when it is appropriate to do so, modify it to fit the characteristics of the students, implement it, and assess its effectiveness can we say he or she has achieved an adequate degree of executive control. A deep rather than superficial understanding is necessary both for the effective use and durability of new skills in one's repertoire. (See Fullan's (1982) discussion of the importance of deep rather than surface understanding.)

Practice in the Workplace

The more new learning that is necessary to transfer the skill into the active repertoire the more the trainee has to be prepared to practice the skill (preferably, as we will see below, with assistance from experts in the skill or from other trainees who are also attempting to integrate it into their active repertoires). We can set forth a number of principles to guide the practice. The first is that practice must follow *immediately* after the attainment of the new skill. If a teacher is learning a new teaching strategy in workshop settings, he or she should practice the new strategy several times under classroom conditions right after the skill has been obtained. If much time elapses before practice in workplace conditions, there will be a serious loss of skill and understanding.

Second, the first practices provide *some* new learning, but the major outcome will be a clear understanding by the teacher of the amount of new learning that is going to be required to achieve full transfer: teaching students to respond to the new strategy, modulating the strategy to accommodate differences in learning styles, changing classroom patterns, and so forth.

Teachers conduct their classrooms by establishing sets of activities and socializing the students to partake in them. They read cues from the students and adjust their behavior in accord with the requirement for that activity flow. A new teaching strategy requires that the teacher obtain new information from the students and modify long-standing patterns of behavior that have become relatively automatic. We estimate that 15 or 20 trials are necessary before this integration takes place to the point where teachers feel nearly as comfortable with a fresh strategy as with their older repertoire.

Both thought processes and deeply ingrained behaviors are triggered by events in the classroom. To the extent that these long-standing behaviors are appropriate to the use of a new skill, they will encourage its integration. However, to the extent that they are not, the teacher will feel uneasy and familiar and comfortable skills will be dislocated as the new strategy is used. After about 15 or 20 trials, a more comfortable state will be reached, however, as greater understanding and skill with the new behaviors provides competence in integrating new repertoire with old.

The Process of Coaching

Setting up arrangements for the trainees to develop a self-help community to provide coaching now is regarded by us as essential if transfer is to be achieved. Ideally, "coaching teams" are developed during training. If we had our way, *all* school faculties would be divided into coaching teams, that is, teams who regularly observe one another's teaching and provide helpful information, feedback, and so forth. In short, we recommend the development of a "coaching environment" in which all personnel see themselves as one another's coaches. For now, however, the primary function of coaching is to assist in the acquisition of new teaching skills. Thus, most of the illustrations that follow will be of teachers organized into coaching teams much like the Inland faculty described in Chapter 1.

What does the process of coaching actually involve? We think it has four major functions:
1. the provision of companionship
2. the provision of technical feedback
3. the analysis of application (extending executive control and attaining "deep" meaning)
4. adaptation to the students.

The provision of companionship. Its first function is to provide interchange with another human being over a difficult process. The coaching relationship results in the possibility of mutual reflection, the checking of perceptions, the sharing of frustrations and successes, and the informal thinking through of mutual problems. Two people, watching each other try a new model of teaching for the first time, will find much to talk about. Companionship provides reassurance that the problems are normal. Both trainees find that their habitual and automatic teaching patterns create awkwardness when they practice the new procedures. Concentrating on unfamiliar moves and ideas, they forget essential little odds and ends. The companionship not only makes the training process technically easier, it enhances the quality of the experience. It is a lot more pleasurable to share a new thing than to do it in isolation. The lonely business of teaching has sorely lacked the companionship that we envision for our coaching teams.

The provision of technical feedback. In the course of training, our team members learn to provide feedback to one another as they practice their new model of teaching. They point out omissions, examine how materials are arranged, check to see whether all parts of the teaching strategy have been brought together, and so on. "Technical" feedback helps ensure that growth continues through practice in the classroom. The pressures of the context tend to diffuse the teaching experience and draw attention away from the new teaching strategy. The provision of technical feedback helps keep the mind of the teacher on the business of perfecting skills, polishing them, and working through problem areas. Nearly any teacher who has been through a training process can learn to provide technical feedback to another teacher.*

The act of providing feedback is also beneficial to the person doing it. The coaching partner has the privilege of seeing a number of trials of the new model by another skilled teacher. It is often easier to see problems of confusion and omission when watching someone else teach than when attempting to recapture one's own process. Ideas about how to use the model are also collected through observation. When a group of four or six teachers observes each other regularly, they not only can give technical feedback to each other, they can receive it vicariously while watching others on the team provide it. Among them, they will also produce a number of fine practices that constitute further demonstrations and from which they can obtain ideas for maximizing their use of the model.

Analysis of application: extending executive control. One of the most important things one learns during the transfer period is when to use a new model appropriately and what will be achieved by doing so. Selecting the right occasions to use a teaching strategy is not as easy as it sounds. Nearly everyone needs help in learning to pick the right spots. Unfamiliar teaching processes also appear to have less certain outcomes than do the familiar ones. From the early trials, one often has the impression that one has "worked all day and not gotten very far." Most of us need help to find out how much we have, in fact, accomplished and, of course, how much we might accomplish by making adjustments in the way we are using the model. During training, the coaching teams need to spend a considerable amount of time examining curriculum materials and plans and practicing the application of the model that they will be using later. Then, as the process of transfer begins, practice in the classroom is intensified, with closer and closer attention given to appropriate use.

Adaptation to the students. As we have already mentioned, much of the energy expended in learning to use a new model of teaching is consumed in the process of learning how to teach it to the children. Successful teaching requires successful student response. Teachers are familiar with the task of

---

*Technical feedback should not be confused with *general evaluation*. Feedback implies no judgment about the overall quality of teaching but is confined to information about the execution of model-relevant skills.

teaching students how to engage in instructional activities that are common. A model that is new to a group of students, however, will cause them trouble. *They* will need to learn new skills and to become acquainted with what is expected of them, how to fulfill the task demands of the new method, and how to gauge their own progress. In addition, the model of teaching needs to be adapted to fit different groups of students. More training must be provided for some, more structure for others, and so on. In the early stages, adaptation to the students is relatively difficult and usually requires a lot of direct assistance and companionship.

One of the major functions of the coach is to help the "players" to "read" the responses of the students so that the right decisions are made about what skill training is needed and how to adapt the model. This is especially important in the early stages of practice when one's hands are full managing one's own behavior and it is more difficult to worry about the students than it will be later on.

When practicing any new approach to teaching, one is surely less competent with it than with the approaches in one's existing repertoire. When trying a new model, nearly all of us feel bad about ourselves as we fumble around. The students sense our uncertainty and let us know in not so subtle ways that they are *aware* we are less certain and sure-footed than usual. At such times, we tend to become easily discouraged. The expression "I tried that method and it didn't work" refers as much to the sense of dismay we feel during the early trials as it does to the actual success or failure of the method itself.

The fact is, successful use of a new method requires practice. The early trials just aren't perfect, or even close to our normal standard of adequacy. One of the principal jobs of the coaching team then is to help its members feel good about themselves during the early trials. It is tragic that teaching currently provides so little interpersonal support and close contact with other teachers, because classrooms are terribly isolated places. Coaching reduces the isolation and offers genuine support.

A question often asked is, who should coach? We're not really sure about that. On a practical basis, most coaching should be done by teams of teachers working together to study new approaches to teaching and to polish their existing teaching skills. There is, of course, no reason why administrators or curriculum supervisors or college professors cannot be effective coaches, too. But if only as a matter of logistics, teachers are closer to one another and in an excellent position to do most of the coaching necessary.

In summary, there are several types of new learning involved in the transfer process. To accomplish these kinds of learning in such a way that they will effectively attack or, better yet, prevent the transfer problem, five techniques are available. These techniques are:

- to forecast the transfer process throughout the training cycle
- to reach the highest possible level of skill development during training

- to develop what we term "executive control," that is, an understanding of the appropriate content for the model and how to adapt it to different types of students—a "meta understanding" about how the model works, how it can be fitted into the instructional repertoire, and how it can be adapted to students
- to practice in the workplace
- to institute a process of coaching during practice in the work setting.

5

Parallels with Athletic Training

We are beginning to discover parallels between the problem of transfer in teaching and the problem of transfer in athletic skills.

There are going to be so many things in your head that your muscles just aren't going to respond like they should for awhile.... You've got to understand that the best way to get through this is to relax, not worry about your mistakes, and come to each practice and each meeting anxious to learn. *We'll generally make you worse before we make you better.*

Coach Rich Brooks of the University of Oregon to his incoming freshman football players, in The Eugene Register-Guard, *August 14, 1981.*

Coach Brooks' recent admonition to his freshmen highlighted the parallels for us. Intrigued, we approached Coach Brooks and asked him to talk with us about training and the problems of transfer. The resulting interview revealed striking similarities in the training problems faced by teachers, football players, and their coaches.

Q. Coach Brooks, I'm interested in how you approach skill development in football training and if you consider the transfer of those skills to game conditions to be a separate training problem.

A. Although our players come to us with skills, we reteach and refine those skills as though we were starting from scratch. We teach them our way of doing it, because all those skills have to fit together into one team. They're all interdependent.

Q. Could you tell me your approach to skill development?

A. We use a part/whole/part method. All skills are broken down into discrete steps. We work on each segment, then combine them into whole skills, then into plays, etc., then go back and work on the specifics of skills that are giving problems.

Q. Could you give me an example of a specific skill and how you would approach the training for that skill?

A. The fundamentals of blocking and tackling—bending the knees and striking a blow. All positions need this skill. The trick is to get the player to visualize, to have a mental picture of how it looks and how it feels. Otherwise, feedback isn't effective. We can tell them where it's wrong, but they can't correct it till they know.

Q. How do you get them "to know" what the skill is?

A. We tell them, show them, demonstrate with people and with film, show them films of themselves, have them practice with the _____ .

Q. The what?

A. It's a mechanical dummy they practice with. We have them practice each move separately, then put the moves together, first one, then two, then three—how their knees should be bent, where their arms should come up, where they strike, what all the muscles should be doing. We diagnose problems with the dummy and keep explaining how it should work, over and over again, in sequence.

Q. In teacher training, we believe that theoretical understanding is important to later performance. How important is it in football skills?

A. It's essential. They must understand how their bodies work, why certain muscle groups in certain combinations achieve certain effects. We never stop explaining.

Q. After they have mastered blocking to your satisfaction with the dummy, then what?

A. Moving from the machine to a live test is difficult; moving from practice to a game is also very difficult. Some people have all the physical ability in the world, all the moves, but can't play because they can't grasp the entire concept, can't fit in with the whole picture.

Q. We have problems with transfer of training, too. Do you coach them differently after they've mastered the "basic skills" of football? What will you be doing differently next month after the season has started? How do you work on transfer?

A. Fear of failure is a factor. My job is to create confidence and success situations. Skills have to be overlearned so that they're past conscious thinking. I can't have someone thinking of how to throw a block in a game. They have to be thinking of who and when and what the guy on their left or behind them is doing.

Q. So specifically, how do you coach transfer of skills to a game situation?

A. First, we re-emphasize skill training for everyone—the second, third, fourth year guys as well. We're always working for improved execution. Then we work hardest on integration, which is just a new kind of teaching. Coaching is really just teaching. We work on confidence by putting them in situations where they can see the improvement. If a guy was lifting 300 pounds two weeks ago and is lifting 350 now, no one has to tell him he's getting stronger.

PARALLELS WITH ATHLETIC TRAINING

Q. How does the training break down for your players right now, before school starts?

A. We spend three hours in the classroom and two hours on the field. On their own, they spend a couple of hours in the weight room and working out and another couple of hours with the trainers, working out their bumps and bruises.

Q. And after school starts?

A. We'll spend 45 minutes a day in class, two hours on the practice field, plus whatever they can manage on their own after studies.

Q. How does that differ from pro football players' training regimen?

A. They meet two-three hours daily in position meetings, offensive and defensive meetings, watching films of themselves and their opponents, then practice two to four hours a day depending on their coaches, then their personal work and time with the trainers. They have more time to get into the complexities of the game.

Changing what we do, even slightly, can unbalance the rest of our "game." Whether we are adjusting the grip on a golf club or initiating an inquiry procedure for science teaching, the new behavior does not fit smoothly with our existing practice. The fact that the new skill may have been perfected in parts and practiced thoroughly in simulated conditions does not prevent the transfer problem. Surrounding behaviors must be adjusted to the presence of a different approach, and the resulting discomfort is often enough to ensure a return to the former smooth, if less efficient, performance.

Perhaps the most striking difference in training between athletes and teachers is the initial assumptions held by each. *Athletes do not believe mastery will be achieved quickly or easily.* They understand that enormous effort will result in small (and not always linear) increments of change. We, on the other hand, have often behaved as though teaching skills were so easily acquired that a simple presentation, one-day workshop, or single videotaped demonstration were sufficient to ensure successful classroom performance. To the extent that we have communicated this message to teachers, we have misled them. Learning to use an inductive strategy in the classroom is surely at least as difficult as learning to throw a block properly.

Coach Brooks' description parallels the argument we have tried to make. The task of learning new skills and integrating them, the knowledge that "we'll generally make you worse before we make you better," and the importance of continuing to try when the results are discouraging eloquently forecast the transfer process. The necessity of overlearning skills to the point that they become automatic if they are to be useful in a more complex setting is also reflected in Brooks' training regimen. "Executive control" is sought in the frequent and ongoing emphasis on theory and the classroom work on "plays," "game plans," and analysis of films.

The elements of coaching in teaching—the provision of companionship and technical feedback, study of application, study of students (or opposing teams) and personal facilitation—are also clear in the interview with Coach Brooks. Football players, however, have a built-in advantage when undertaking this process: their training is *organized* as a group activity with continuous feedback from coaches. We came away from this interview feeling more strongly than ever that teachers must also organize *themselves* into groups for the express purpose of training themselves and each other and to facilitate the transition from skill development to transfer.

6
Increasing Learning Aptitude

To increase one's repertoire is to develop the aptitude to teach: the ability to coordinate objectives, students, and learning environments with increasing skill and effectiveness. Moreover, the more we develop our repertoire, the more we develop the ability to *add* to that repertoire *at will*.

The most important outcome of any educational exercise is an increase in aptitude—the ability to learn in new situations and to solve problems as they arise. Academic subjects provide us with examples. As a student learns skills in arithmetic, those skills represent an increased aptitude to solve problems, including sizing them up, sorting out the important features of the situation, selecting which skills to use, and applying them. Learning new skills increases one's aptitude to solve problems. Similarly, the well-developed reader has the aptitude to read new things, that is, material not previously encountered. Previously acquired knowledge of literature is brought to bear on new literary works. The primary importance of instruction in reading is not the material read in class but the increased aptitude it gives the student to handle new material.

The purpose of training for teachers is to increase the aptitude to learn in new situations, that is, to comprehend and solve goal-related problems. We try to increase our repertoire of teaching strategies so we can more effectively select objectives, pick appropriate models of teaching, and adjust them to the learning requirements of our students (Hunt, 1971). As we organize training, it is our goal not only to provide environments that maximize teachers' opportunities to expand their repertoire but also to increase their ability to learn new skills and apply them as they teach. Essentially, the more we learn the easier it becomes.

We believe that the research on training conducted in the last 20 years has yielded enormous dividends. We understand better both the nature of transfer and the problem of achieving it, and we are able to outline procedures to enable nearly all teachers to learn the most powerful teaching strategies to the point where they can use them comfortably in the classroom. Working in teams committed to the coaching process, teachers can explore the theory behind any given teaching strategy, examine demonstrations, practice and provide one another feedback, and coach one another through the process of application.

An optimal training program is also organized so that the tasks of adding to the teaching repertoire become easier and easier—that is, the teachers not only acquire new teaching strategies but become better and better at the process of learning them. We are beginning to understand something about how to do this and have developed a series of propositions to guide program construction when increasing one's aptitude to learn is an objective.

Principle 1: Learning new teaching strategies in itself increases the ability to learn other ones. In other words, engaging in the training process itself has beneficial effects. When teachers participate in a program designed to teach them several new teaching strategies, the first one is the hardest, the second one somewhat easier, and the third and fourth much easier than the first two. We can discover why this is true by considering a group of typical experienced teachers engaging in a program designed to help them learn new teaching strategies for the first time.

As the first model of teaching is presented, some members of the group are relatively indifferent to the theory of the model, while others watch the demonstration somewhat critically and spend much of the discussion time questioning whether the teaching strategy will in fact be of value to them. Still others resist the practice sessions, believing that a few demonstrations and a little explanation are "all we need" in order to use the teaching strategy. A few others are resistant to feedback and, finally, some of the coaching teams are slow getting started and some members of the coaching teams are slow to begin the necessary practice.

By the time the second model rolls around, however, the value of the theory is more clear and the demonstrations are watched more closely because everyone knows that practice will follow soon thereafter. Feedback is more welcome, practice less resisted. In fact, they have discovered that the process of teaching for one another is rather enjoyable and not nearly as threatening as it seemed. Feedback is also welcomed because the importance of a high level of skill development has become clear. The coaching teams have also become organized, and the importance of early practice is now apparent to everyone. In other words, practice in the training process increases one's skill in engaging in it. In fact, when teams stay together, they often worked out ways to make the process more efficient. For all these reasons, experience with the training process increases the aptitude to profit from it.

Principle 2: The more highly skilled learners understand the process of transfer better. Hence, the study of the process of transfer should become part of the content of training.

In our own training, we incorporate the content of this piece directly into the training program. As the coaching teams are organized, the process of transfer is discussed—forecast, as we put it above—and the research base for the training program is laid out in detail.

We find that the analogies from the sports, business, and military worlds are useful because they help teachers visualize the transfer problem as a general one rather than something specific to teaching. Direct experience with the transfer problem, however, remains the most useful teacher, and we try to accomplish this in two ways. First, we organize the training so that the first goal is to acquire a relatively simple teaching skill, and the training components are employed to help the trainees acquire that skill. The skill of "explaining" is a useful example, and the following sequence is generally employed.

First, each teacher is given a written passage about an unfamiliar topic and provided some time to study it and prepare a brief (two- or three-minute) explanation of the topic for a group of peers. Working in small groups, each trainee explains the major points in the passage he or she has been given with a time limit placed on the explanation. Nearly everyone finds that it is much harder to explain a topic than they first believed. The skills for explaining are then described and some brief demonstrations are given. Then the process is repeated. Each person receives a new written passage, studies it, and then again attempts to explain it to a small group of peers. Performance increases, but nearly everyone is still dissatisfied with his or her explanation. The cycle is then repeated two or three times with further explanations of explaining and more practice. By the end of a single day, nearly all of the teachers are surprised at their increase in skill and comfort, although prior to the day nearly every one of them would probably have asserted that he or she was a relative expert at "explaining."

Exercises such as these are persuasive, but they are not enough. The more powerful experience occurs as the first model of teaching is taught, and the coaching teams find themselves engaged directly in the problem of transfer. They find that the research does indeed accurately depict the problem and that nearly everyone has to work very hard through a serious period of discomfort before gradually beginning to achieve some mastery of the model.

Principle 3: The process is simplified by concentrating on over-learning: first the new skill, then "first-stage" application, and then "expanded control." The entire training process is not satisfying to teachers until complete mastery has been achieved. Most teachers are quite frustrated until that point has been reached. Once teachers understand the training problem, however, they become much more comfortable with focusing first on the essential skills of the new teaching approach, then on finding opportunities to initially apply it without expecting full mastery, and only after that on getting assistance to help them achieve full control.

For most of us, the attempt to reach full control in the first stage is simply unrealistic. We need to concentrate on the basics, get enough experience with the new skills so they become relatively comfortable, and then concentrate on understanding how to use the model and adapt it to students. With increasing experience, teachers become much more comfortable concentrating on each of these levels of control in turn and become less frustrated when the last level cannot be achieved completely.

This also helps teachers overcome what we call a "batting away" reflex at the onset of discomfort during training. For many trainees, the first reaction to the use of a new skill is the relative awkwardness of that skill in comparison with long-standing ones. There is a tendency to reject the skill at that point and to begin to resist the training. But with experience and the acquisition of new skills, teachers become more understanding of their own discomfort and more receptive to attempts to help ease their passage through the initial stages of training.

Trainers need to understand that this discomfort is normal and accept it. Many good training programs have been discarded because the trainers, having discovered a really fine approach to teaching, mistakenly lose faith in the idea when it meets with resistance from the trainees. But the idea itself is seldom being rejected. The trainees are going through a normal process of discomfort that will gradually disappear as the training is consolidated.

Principle 4: The greatest new learning occurs with engagement with unfamiliar skills. There is a perverse law of training that everyone needs to understand. It is simply that the more important an addition to one's repertoire a given model of teaching is, the greater the discomfort it will cause. The greatest opportunity for all of us as teachers is to learn skills that are quite unfamiliar to us but which have the most potential when we apply them in the classroom. We stretch ourselves by reaching out beyond the edges of our contemporary repertoire. Teachers and trainers alike have a tendency to seek the teaching skills that will be most easily acquired, that is, ones adjacent to or well within our contemporary range. But as training progresses, we come to understand that the greatest new learning pulls at the edges of our current range of skills and takes us to places where our initial discomfort will be succeeded by a true addition to our aptitude to solve the problems of teaching.

States of Growth

Nothing is more important to a human being's health than his or her ability to continue to grow and adapt. No profession magnifies that truth more than education. The teacher's life is one of changing conditions: new students, new ideas, and social ferment. Adaptation is essential. There is no endeavor where lack of growth is more clearly and desperately damaging than teaching.

While the enormous importance of personal and professional states of growth has long been recognized, in the ebb and flow of research and practice it has received varying degrees of attention. In the last few years, however, it has again begun to receive a lot of attention, partly because of concern about the nature of "adult learners," partly through studies of adult continuing education, and partly as a result of recent studies of teachers' self-concepts and interactions with their environments.

Recent studies (McKibbin and Joyce, 1982) have begun to identify clear differences among teachers when they interact with the formal system of staff development, with one another, and with the environments of their personal lives. As is the case with all other groups of people, some teachers are in states of very active interchange with their environments while others are less active, isolated from, and even resistant to opportunities for growth.

The mastery of complex academic content and new teaching strategies requires an active state of interchange. The periods of discomfort to be gone through, the continuing interaction with colleagues essential to successful training, and coaching others to become honest and strong require active learning states. Collaborative governance of training directly increases motivation and involvement and generates several conditions conducive to achievement (Joyce, ed., 1978). Critical is the creation of a productive social system so that those in the most active states of growth help others to reach out more powerfully into their environments. The key is in the development of an energizing environment within the workplace of teachers.

In McKibbin and Joyce's (1982) recent study of the growth states of more than 200 teachers, it became clear that a substantial portion of them were heavily influenced by the environment of their school, some positively, some negatively. Many teachers who otherwise would have been "passive consumers" were propelled into more active states because the social climate of their school was active and compelling. In less active environments, some of the most energized teachers worked in relative isolation, generating their own social climate with small groups of peers. Many of those in less active states became withdrawn and in some cases resistant. Sharan and Hertz-Lazarowitz (1982) have documented clearly the effect of resistance on training. In a loose and disorganized social climate without clear goals, reticent teachers may actually subvert elements of the training process not only for themselves but also for others.

Unquestionably, principals can have a substantial effect on the social climate of their schools, both by direct leadership and by freeing the energy of the more active teachers and increasing their influence within the social system of the school. Powerful training of the type we have been describing is exceptionally difficult to implement except in energized environments.

Adaptation of Training to the Learning Styles of Teachers

Training need not be seen as a monolithic series of steps. Teachers have preferences for varying degrees of control over their own activities. Their conceptual level and self-concept interact with their training (Showers, 1982). Training that is inflexible will perforce generate negative energy by depressing motivation and creating dissidence between trainees and trainers. Caring and considerate instructional designers and trainers can create settings in which training is modulated to the learning style of the teacher. The energizing qualities of the environment and the states of growth of the teachers involved enormously influence both one's satisfaction with training and its likelihood of success. Responsive environments permit teachers to influence the process of training and adapt it to significant differences in their learning styles.

We are confident that effective training procedures exist. They should be implemented in such a way that the social environment of teaching becomes more adoptive and energizing, pulling teachers toward more active states of growth, providing avenues that release the power of individual styles of learning, and enabling teachers to increase their own personal technology for acquiring fresh ideas and skills.

Appendix

In this Appendix we have reviewed the literature on teacher training and curriculum implementation that formed the basis for the ideas and findings reported in this monograph. Our concern about transfer of training guided both the selection and organization of the studies included in this review. Table 1 summarizes a series of studies concerning questions raised by people skeptical about whether teachers can in fact learn new and alternative teaching strategies. Specifically, these studies addressed such questions as:

1. Given intensive training, including the study of the rationale of new models, demonstration or modeling of them, practice and feedback with them, and demand for them in the classroom, can teachers become proficient with teaching models not existing in their previous repertoire?
2. Are "natural" teaching styles relevant to the acquisition of new models? That is, can generally nondirective teachers learn nondirective models more quickly than relatively directive persons?
3. How does personality (especially conceptual level) affect the acquisition of particular models?
4. How do ideological preferences affect the acquisition of new teaching strategies?
5. Can teachers using models they have been taught generate student outcomes appropriate to the models being used?

By the mid-1970s (see Table 1) these studies had demonstrated that most preservice and inservice teacher candidates could acquire a number of models of teaching provided that they received intensive training, that higher conceptual level (CL) teachers acquired additional repertoire more easily than low CL teachers, that there was little if any relationship between natural teaching styles and the acquisition of any particular model, that ideological preferences generally had a minimal effect on model acquisition, and, finally, that skill training appeared to be model-specific rather than acting as a generic facilitator.

However, although these studies did not address the problem specifically, reports from the hundreds of teachers who participated in the studies indicated a wide variation in the transfer from training into regular and active use

Table 1. Models of Teaching Training Systems: Selected Related Research.

Focus of Study	Investigator (Date)	Models Investigated	Independent Variables	Dependent Variables (Measures)	Sample	Results	Comments
Training Elements	O'Donnell (1974)	Advance Organizer Synectics	Training: Theory, Demonstration, Practice, Feedback	Skill in Model Performance (Clinical Analysis, Interaction Analysis)	30 preservice candidates	90% of subjects performed models at acceptable levels	Tested effectiveness of training paradigm to level.
	Joyce, Weil, Wald (1981)	Concept Attainment Synectics Group Investigation	Training: Theory, Demonstration, Practice, Feedback Personality: Conceptual Level Natural Teaching Style	Skill in Model Performance (Clinical Analysis, Interaction Analysis)	30 preservice candidates	Teaching behavior shifted in appropriate directions when attempting to use models	Conceptual level influenced style but did not inhibit training effects Characteristics of normal teaching style did not affect training results
	Kelly (1973)	Repertories of Four Models	Training: Theory, Demonstration, Practice, Feedback Natural Teaching Style	Skill in Model Performance (Clinical Analysis, Interaction Analysis)	30 inservice teachers	Teacher displayed skills of models for "on call" observations	Teachers varied in voluntary use of models
	Brown (1967)	Repertoire of Models	Training: Theory, Demonstration, Practice,		30 teachers	Acquisiton of repertoire displayed in "on call"	Need for coaching apparent

APPENDIX

Tinsman (1971)	Three Strategies	Training: Feedback, over 30 weeks Personality: Conceptual Level Demonstrates: Three Styles	30 preservice candidates	observations. Personality related to natural styles. Feedback only relatively ineffective in changing styles Personality related to "natural" styles Demonstration effective in inducing model skills
		Feedback Personality: Conceptual Level		Need for modelling established. Confirms research by others (Table Three) Ease of acquisition of new skills with intensive modelling-feedback treatment established
Murphy and Brown (1970)	As Repertoire	Training, Utilization of the theory demonstration, feedback Personality: conceptual level	30 home economics teachers	Skill and Model Performance (Clinical Analysis, Interaction Analysis)
				Acquisiton of repertoire displayed in on-call observations. Personality related to natural styles and acquisition of models.
				Applicability to preparation of home economics teacher demonstrated.
McKibbin & Joyce, 1980	A repertoire of eight models	Training with an emphasis on coaching	20 inservice teachers	Transfer of Model into Repertoire
				Psychological states relevant to transfer
				The need for intensive coaching especially of teacher of low CL

in one's repertoire. Thus, while these studies addressed concerns expressed by many teacher educators, they did not provide a solution to our fundamental paradox: we appear to be able to provide conditions that enable teachers to acquire complex models of teaching, but many of these teachers do not employ these models in the regular and thoughtful way that was intended.

Analysis of Teacher Training Studies

Criteria for inclusion of studies in this review included independent variables that could be construed as training and the measurement of dependent variables that represented training outcomes. Many of the studies retrieved through computer searches of the literature were discarded (for purposes of this review) because training elements were not specified, the results of the training were not measured, or they employed such brief or weak treatments that conclusions could not be confidently drawn.

The 56 studies that remained after this screening were then categorized by the outcomes achieved: changes in teachers' knowledge and/or attitudes (Table 2), skill acquisition (Table 3), teachers' abilities to transfer skills in a horizontal or lateral sense (Table 4), and teachers' vertical transfer of skills to classroom practice (Table 5). For example, if a training study attempted to develop skills in trainees but accomplished only a more positive attitude toward the new behavior, it is reported in Table 2 (knowledge/attitudes) rather than in Table 3 (skill acquisition). When, because of measurement or design flaws, outcomes appeared to be achieved but the strength of a casual relationship was questionable, the possible outcomes are indicated with a question mark. Finally, when single studies employed multiple treatments, effects are shown for each treatment.

After choosing the appropriate table on which to report each study, all the studies were further identified by:
1. The Content of Training—*FT*, fine tuning of existing skills, or *NR*, content that represented new repertoire for trainees experiencing the training
2. The Outcomes Sought by the Training—*knowledge, skills, horizontal transfer*, or *vertical transfer*
3. The Training Elements Included—presentation of *theory*, *demonstrations* of the behavior to be acquired, opportunities for *practice* and *feedback*, and the *coaching* of teachers in their classrooms as they attempt the mastery and implementation of recently acquired skills and behaviors.

The presentation does not take into account the length of treatment, which is probably an important variable in the acquisition of skills and transfer of training. The inclusion of length of training as a classification variable in future analyses of training research should more vividly demonstrate the efficacy of extensive training programs for acquisition and transfer of teaching skills and strategies.

APPENDIX

Table 2. Training Studies: Knowledge Acquisition.

Study	Content of Training			Outcomes Sought				Training Elements Included						Outcomes Achieved			
	FT	NR	Know	Skill	HT	VT	T	D	P	F	C	Know	Skill	HT	VT
Cruickshank, 1968		X	X			X	X		X	X		X			
Popham, 1966		X	X	X			X	X	X			X			
Kepler, 1977	X		X	X	X					X		?	?		
Koran, 1969		X	X	X		X	X		X			X			
Koran, 1970		X	X	X		?	X	X	X			X			
							X		X	X		X			
Gliessman & Pugh, 1978	X		X	X			X	X				X	X		
Vlcek, 1966	X		X	X	X		X		X			X	?		
Galloway & Mickelson, 1973		X	X	X			X		X			X	?		

Table 3. Training Studies: Skill Acquisition.

Study	Content of Training FT	Content of Training NR	Outcomes Sought Know	Outcomes Sought Skill	Outcomes Sought HT	Outcomes Sought VT	Training Elements Included T	Training Elements Included D	Training Elements Included P	Training Elements Included F	Training Elements Included C	Outcomes Achieved Know	Outcomes Achieved Skill	Outcomes Achieved HT	Outcomes Achieved VT
Alssid & Hutchinson, 1979	x						x					x	x		
Bell, 1970	x		x	x	x		x			x		x	x		
Borg, 1977	x		x	x	x		x					x	x		
Borg et al., 1969	x		x	x			x	x	x			x	x		
Charles, 1980		x	x	x	x		x	x	x	x		x	x		
Collins, 1978	x		x	x					x			x	x		
DeTure, 1979	x		x	x				x	x	x		x	x		
Edwards, 1975	x		x	x			x		x	x		x	x		
Friebel & Kallenbach, 1969	x		x	x	x		x	x	x	x		x	x		
Koran, Snow, & McDonald, 1971	x		x	x	x		x	x	x			?			
Orme, 1966	x		x		x		x	x	x			x	x		
Perkins & Atkinson, 1973						x	x								
Riley, 1978	x		x	x	x		x		x	x		x	x		
	x		x	x					x			x	x		
Ronnestad, 1977		x	x						x	x		x	x		
							x	x	x			?			
Rosenthal, 1977		x	x		x		x		x	x		x	x		
							x					x	x		
Sadker & Sadker, 1975		?	x				x		x			x	x		
Santiestedban & Koran, 1977			x	x			x	x	x	x		x	x	x	
Stone & Geppert, 1979	x		x	x	x		x	x	x			x	x	x	
	x						x								

Table 4. Training Studies: Horizontal Transfer of Knowledge/Skills.

Study	Content of Training		Outcomes Sought				Training Elements Included						Outcomes Achieved			
	FT	NR	Know	Skill	HT	VT	T	D	P	F	C		Know	Skill	HT	VT
Ascione & Borg, 1980	X	?	X	X	X		X		X	X			X	X	1/2	
Bondi, 1970		X	X	X	X		X	X	X	X			X	X	2/3	
Borg, 1975	X		X	X	X	X	X		X	X			X	X	X*	
Borg, 1977	X		X	X	X	X	X	X	X	X			X	X	X*	
Borg, Langer, & Kelly, 1969	X		X	X	X	X	X	X	X	X			X	X	X*	
Copeland, 1977	X		X	X	X		X	X	X	X			X	X	X	
Dansereau et al., 1979		X	X	X	X	X	X		X				X	X	X*	
Feldens & Duncan, 1978	X		X	X	X	?	X		X	X	?		X	X	X	
Good & Grouws, 1979	X		X	X	X	?	X		X	X			X	X	X	
Johnson & Sloat, 1980	X	?	X	X	X	X	X	X	X	X	?		X	X	X	
Kallenbach & Gall, 1969	X		X	X	X	X	X	X	X	X			X	X	X	
Spooner & Stone, 1977	X		X	X	X		X		X	X			X	?	X	
Stallings, 1979	X	X	X	X	X	X	X	X	X				X	X	X	?
Stokes & Keys, 1978		X	X	X	X		X	X	X				X	X	X	
Yeany, 1977	X		X	X	X	X	X	X	X				X	X	—	?
Zevin, 1973		X	X	X	X	X	X	X	X				?	?		

*Vertical transfer may have been achieved.

Table 5. Training Studies: Vertical Transfer of Knowledge/Skills.

Study	Contents of Training			Outcomes Sought				Training Elements Included					Outcomes Achieved			
	FT	NR		Know	Skill	HT	VT	T	D	P	F	C	Know	Skill	HT	VT
Baker, 1983		X		X	X	X	X	X	X	X	X	X	X	X	X	X
Good & Bruphy, 1974	X			X	X	X	X	X			X		X	X	X	X
Jacobson, 1977		X		X	X	X	X	X		X	X		X	X	X	X
Mohlman, 1981	X			X	X	X	X	X	X	X	X		X	X	X	
Moore & Schaut, 1978-9		X		X	X	X	X	X		X	X	X	X	X	X	X
Sharon & Hertz-Lazarowitz, 1982		X		X	X	X	X	X	X	X	X	X	X	X	X	X
Showers, 1982		X		X	X	X	X	X	X		X	X	X	X	X	X

References

Alssid, L.L., and Hutchinson, W.R. "Comparison for Modeling Techniques in Counselor Training." *Counselor Education and Supervision* (1977): 36-41.

Arends, Richard I. "Beginning Teacher as Learner." Paper presented to the American Educational Research Association, New York City, 1982.

Ascione, F.R., and Borg, W.R. "Effects of a Training Program on Teacher Behavior and Handicapped Children's Self-Concepts." *The Journal of Psychology* 104 (1980): 53-65.

Baker, R.G. "The Contribution of Coaching to Transfer of Training: An Extension Study." Unpublished dissertation, University of Oregon, 1983.

Bell, C.G. "Can the Art of Teaching be Structured?" *Journal of Home Economics* 62 (1970): 34-39.

Bondi, J.C., Jr. "Feedback From Interaction Analysis: Some Implications for the Improvement of Teaching." *Journal of Teacher Education* 21 (1970): 189-196.

Borg, W.R. "Protocol Materials as Related to Teacher Performance and Pupil Achievement." *Journal of Educational Research* 69 (1975): 23-30.

Borg, W.R. "Changing Teacher and Pupil Performance With Protocols." *Journal of Experimental Education* 45 (1975); 9-18.

Borg, W.R., and others. "Videotape Feedback and Microteaching in a Teacher Training Model." *Journal of Experimental Education* 37 (1969): 9-16.

Borg, W.R.; Langer, R.; and Kelley, M.L. "The Minicourse: A New Tool for the Education of Teachers." *Education* (1969): 232-238.

Brown, Clark. "A Multivariate Study of the Teaching Styles of Student Teachers." Doctoral dissertation, Teachers College, Columbia University, 1967.

Charles, R.I. "Exemplification and Characterization Moves in the Classroom Teaching of Geometry Concepts." *Journal for Research in Mathematics Education* 11 (1980): 10-21.

Collins, M.L. "Effects of Enthusiasm Training on Preservice Elementary Teachers." *Journal of Teacher Education* 29 (1978): 53-57.

Copeland, W.D. "Some Factors Related to Student Teacher Classroom Performance Following Microteaching Training." *American Educational Research Journal* 14 (1977): 147-157.

Cruikshank, D.P. "Simulation." *Theory Into Practice* 7 (1968): 190-193.

Dansereau, D.F., and others. "Development and Evaluation of a Learning Strategy Training Program." *Journal of Educational Psychology* 71 (1979): 64-73.

DeTure, L.R. "Relative Effects of Modeling on the Acquisition of Wait-Time by Preservice Elementary Teachers and Concomitant Changes in Dialogue Patterns." *Journal of Research in Science Teaching* 16 (1979): 553-562.

Edwards, C.H. "Changing Teacher Behavior Through Self Instruciton and Supervised Micro Teaching in a Competency Based Program." *Journal of Educational Research* 68 (1975): 219-222.

Feldens, M., and Duncan, J. "A Field Experiment: Teacher-Directed Changes in Instructional Behavior." *Journal of Teacher Education* 29 (1978): 47-51.

Friebel, A.C., and Kallenbach, W.W. "Effects of Videotape Feedback and Microteaching as Developed in the Field Test of Minicourse I with Student Teachers." Paper presented at the California Educational Research Association, Los Angeles, March 15, 1969.

Fullan, Michael. *The Meaning of Educational Change.* New York: Teachers College Press, 1982.

Gall, Meredith D. *The Relationship Between Inservice Education Practices and Effectiveness of Basic Skills Instruction.* Final Report. Eugene, Ore.: Center for Educational Policy and Management, December 1982.

Galloway, C.G., and Mickelson, N.I. "Improving Teachers' Questions." *Elementary School Journal* 74 (1973): 145-148.

Gliessman, D., and Pugh, R.C. "Acquiring Teacher Behavior Concepts Through the Use of High-Structure Protocol Films." *Journal of Educational Psychology* 70 (1978): 779-787.

Good, T.L., and Brophy, J.E. "An Emperical Investigation: Changing Teacher and Student Behavior." *Journal of Educational Psychology* 66 (1974): 399-405.

Good, T.L., and Grouws, D.A. "Teaching and Mathematics Learning." *Educational Leadership* 37 (1979): 39-45.

Hunt, David. *Matching Models in Education.* Toronto: Ontario Institute for Studies in Education, 1971.

Johnson, J.L., and Sloat, K.C. "Teacher Training Effects: Real or Illusory?" *Psychology in the Schools* 17 (1980): 109-115.

Joyce, Bruce R., ed. *Involvement: A Study of Shared Governance of Teacher Education.* Syracuse: National Dissemination Center, 1978.

Joyce, Bruce R., and Clift, Renee. "Generic Training Problems: Training Elements, Socialization, Contextual Variables, and Personality Disposition Across Occupational Categories that Vary in Ethos." Paper presented at the annual meeting of the American Educational Research Association, Montreal, April 11-15, 1983.

Joyce, Bruce R.; Bush, R.N.; and McKibbin, Michael. *Information and Opinion From the California Staff Development Study.* Palo Alto, Calif.: Booksend Laboratories, 1982.

Joyce, Bruce R.; Hersh, Richard; and McKibbin, Michael. *The Structure of School Improvement.* New York: Longman, Inc., 1983.

Joyce, Bruce R., and Showers, Beverly. "Teacher Training Research: Working Hypotheses for Program Design and Questions for Further Study." Paper presented to the American Educational Research Association, Los Angeles, 1981.

Joyce, Bruce R., and Showers, Beverly. "The Coaching of Teaching." *Educational Leadership* 40 (October 1982): 4-10.

Joyce, Bruce R., and Weil, Marsha. *Models of Teaching,* 2nd ed. Englewood Cliffs, N.J.: Prentice-Hall, Inc., 1980.

Joyce, B.R.; Weil, M.; and Wald, R. "The Teacher Innovator: Models of Teaching as the Core of Teacher Education." *Interchange* 4 (1974): 47-60.

Jacobson, N.S. "Problem Solving and Contingency Contracting in the Treatment of Marital Discord." *Journal of Consulting and Clinical Psychology* 45 (1977): 92-100.

Kallenbach, W.W., and Gall, M.D. "Microteaching Versus Conventional Methods in Training Elementary Intern Teachers." *Journal of Educational Research* 63 (1969): 136-141.

Kelley, J. "An Analysis of the Moves Made by Elementary School Teachers in Operationalizing Two Theory-Based Teaching Models." Unpublished doctoral dissertation, Teachers College, Columbia University, 1973.

Kepler, K.B. "Descriptive Feedback: Increasing Teacher Awareness, Adapting Research Techniques." Paper presented at the annual meeting of the American Educational Research Association, New York City, 1977.

Koran, J.J., Jr. "The Relative Effects of Classroom Instruction and Subsequent Observational Learning on the Acquisition of Questioning Behavior by Pre-Service Elementary Science Teachers." *Journal of Research in Science Teaching* 6 (1969): 217-223.

Koran, J.J., Jr. "A Comparison of the Effects of Observational Learning and Self-Rating on the Acquisition and Retention of a Questioning Behavior by Elementary Science Teacher Trainees." *Science Education* 54 (1970): 385-389.

Koran, M.L.; Snow, R.E.; and McDonald, F. "Teacher Aptitude and Observational Learning of a Teaching Skill." *Journal of Educational Psychology* 62 (1971): 219-228.

Leithwood, K.A., and Montgomery, D.J. "The Role of the Elementary School Principal in Program Development." *Review of Educational Research* 52 (1982): 309-339.

Lortie, Dan. *Schoolteacher.* Chicago: University of Chicago Press, 1975.

McKibbin, Michael, and Joyce, Bruce R. "Psychological States and Staff Development." *Theory Into Practice* 19 (Autumn 1980): 248-255.

Mertens, Sally, and Yarger, Sam *Teacher Center in Action.* Syracuse: Syracuse Area Teacher Center, 1981.

REFERENCES

Miles, Matthew. "Mapping the Common Properties of Schools." In *Improving Schools: Using What We Know*. Edited by Rolf Lehming and Michael Kane. Beverly Hills, Calif.: Sage Publications, Inc., 1981.

Mohlman, Georgea G. "Assessing the Impact of Three Inservice Teacher Training Models." Paper presented at the annual meeting of the American Educational Research Association, New York City, 1982.

Moore, J.W., and Schaut, J.A. "Increasing Instructional Effectiveness Through the Use of a Problem-Solving Approach to the Design of Instructional Systems." *Journal of Experimental Education* 47 (1978-79): 156-161.

Murphy, P.D., and Brown, M. "Conceptual Systems and Teaching Styles." *American Educational Research Journal* 7 (1980): 519-540.

O'Donnell, K. "Natural Teaching Styles and Models of Teaching." Unpublished doctoral dissertation, Teachers College, Columbia University, 1974.

Orme, M. "The Effects of Modeling and Feedback Variables on the Acquisition of a Complex Teaching Strategy." Unpublished doctoral dissertation, Stanford University, 1966.

Perkins, S.R., and Atkinson, D.R. "Effect of Selected Techniques for Training Resident Assistants in Human Relations Skills." *Journal of Counseling Psychology* 20 (1973): 81-90.

Popham, W. James. "Instructional Video Tapes in Teacher Education." *AV Communication Review* 14 (1966): 371-376.

Riley, J.P., II. "Effects of Studying a Question Classification System on the Cognitive Level of Preservice Teachers' Questions." *Science Education* 62 (1978): 333-338.

Ronnestad, M.H. "The Effects of Modeling, Feedback, and Experiential Methods on Counselor Empathy." *Counselor Education and Supervision* 16 (1977): 194-201.

Rosenthal, N.R. "A Prescriptive Approach for Counselor Training." *Journal of Counseling Psychology* 24 (1977): 231-237.

Ryan, Kevin. *Biting the Apple*. New York: Longman, 1980.

Sadker, M., and Sadker, D. "Microteaching for Affective Skills." *Elementary School Journal* 76 (1975): 90-99.

Santiesteban, A.J., and Koran, J.J., Jr. "Acquisition of Science Teaching Skills Through Psychological Modeling and Concomitant Student Learning." *Journal of Research in Science Teaching* 14 (1977): 199-207.

Sharan, Schlomo, and Hertz-Lazarowitz, Rachel. "Effects on an Instructional Change Program on Teachers' Behavior, Attitudes, and Perceptions." *The Journal of Applied Behavioral Science* 18 (1982): 185-201.

Showers, Beverly. *Transfer of Training: The Contribution of Coaching*. Final Report. Eugene, Ore.: Center for Educational Policy and Management, University of Oregon, 1982.

Spooner, Sue E., and Stone, Shelley C. "Maintenance of Specific Counseling Skills Over Time." *Journal of Counseling Psychology* 24 (1977): 66-71.

Stallings, J. *How to Change the Process of Teaching Reading in Secondary Schools*. Menlo Park, Calif.: SRI International, 1979.

Stokes, J.P., and Keys, C.B. "Design and Evaluation of a Short-Term Para-Professional Training Program." *Counselor Education and Supervision* 17 (1978): 279-285.

Stone, C.I., and Geppert, C.C. "Job-Interviewing Skills Training: An Empirical Investigation of Two Methods." *Rehabilitation Counseling Bulletin* (June 1979): 396-401.

Tinsman, S. "The Effects of Instructional Flexibility Training on Teaching Styles and Controlled Repertoire." In *Flexibility in Teaching*. Edited by B. Joyce, C. Clark, and L. Peck. New York: Longman, 1981.

Vlcek, C. "Classroom Simulation in Teacher Education." *Audio-Visual Instruction* 11 (1966): 86-90.

Yeeny, R., Jr. "The Effects of Model Viewing with Systematic Strategy Analysis on the Science Teaching Styles of Preservice Teachers." *Journal of Research in Science Teaching* 14 (1977): 209-222.

Zevin, J. "Training Teachers in Inquiry." *Social Education* 37 (1973): 310-316.

Also of interest . . .

For further exploration of staff development, readers may find the following ASCD media useful:

Publications

	Price	Quantity

Readings in Educational Supervision. Edith E. Grimsley and Ray E. Bruce, editors. A collection of readings from *Educational Leadership* on nine topics including the supervisor as leader in staff development. 1982. 201 pp. (611-82272) — **$9.00** _____

Selecting Learning Experiences: Linking Theory and Practice. Bruce R. Joyce. Uses both theory and practice in discussing the process of matching the student's learning style with the appropriate teaching model. 1978. 55 pp. (611-78138) — **$4.75** _____

Staff Development. Theme issue of *Educational Leadership*. Characteristics and examples of effective training and development programs for teachers, including an interview with David Berliner. October 1982. 80 pp. (611-82274) — **$3.00** _____

Staff Development/Organization Development. Betty Dillon-Peterson, editor. Treats self-renewal by interweaving change in the individual with change in the organization. Discusses the unique characteristics of the adult learner, a five-stage model for effective inservice, and the evaluation process. 1981 Yearbook. 149 pp. (610-81232) — **$9.75** _____

Staff Development: Staff Liberation. Charles W. Beegle and Roy A. Edelfelt, editors. Presents a variety of ways of conceptualizing and organizing the staff improvement function, emphasizing the "liberation" and self-growth of individuals. 1977. 124 pp. (611-77106) — **$6.50** _____

Audiocassettes

                                                 Price   *Quantity*

Peer Supervision: An Alternative. Alan E. Simon. The principal of a school in which teachers successfully use the clinical supervision model explains how the program works. 1979. (612-22310)   **$6.50**   _____

The Stages of Teaching: New Perspectives on Staff Development for Teachers' Needs. Kevin Ryan and others. 1979. (612-20197)   **$9.00**   _____

What Research Says about Inservice Education. Bruce R. Joyce. 1977. 45 min. (612-20172)   **$6.50**   _____

Special discount of 25% off the retail price when purchasing all eight media items!

Ordering and Payment Information
1. Indicate on the form the quantity of each item you wish to order.
2. Please be sure your name and address appear below.
3. All orders totaling $20 or less must be accompanied by payment. ASCD absorbs the cost of postage and handling on all prepaid orders. Make checks or money order payable to ASCD.
4. If order is to billed, postage and handling are extra.
5. Orders from institutions and businesses must be on an official purchase order form.

Mail to: **Please check form of payment:**
ASCD   ____ Enclosed is my check or
Dept. 1113   money order in the
Alexandria, VA 22314   amount of $ _____
(703) 549-9110   ____ Please bill me (postage and handling extra)

Name _____

Address _____

_____

City _____ **State** _____ **Zip** _____